Up the Down Elevator

Norma Farber

illustrations by Annie Gusman

 **Addison-Wesley**

39322

For the little Fishes, Erica and Warren
N.F.

For Lee and Gus
A.G.

When the elevator stopped at **1**
a baker got on with a hot cross bun,
up the down elevator.

When the elevator stopped at **2**
a chef got on with a crocodile stew,
and a blacksmith mending a stallion's shoe,
up the down elevator.

When the elevator stopped at **3**
a waitress got on with a tea ball of tea,
and a sailor in black with a breeze of the sea,
and an animal trainer training a flea,
    up the down elevator.

When the elevator stopped at **4**
a golfer got on, crying Fore!Fore!Fore!,
and a doorman revolving a circular door,
a trumpeter playing a symphony score,
and a busboy with forty-four dishes or more,
up the down elevator.

When the elevator stopped at **5**
a bee-man got on with a honeybee hive,
and a milkman with cows,
a farmer with ploughs,
a shepherd with flocks,
a locksmith with locks,
    up the down elevator.

When the elevator stopped at **6**

a mason got on with a barrow of bricks,

and a miner with picks,

a poultryman with chicks,

a magician with tricks,

a gardener with flowers,

a weatherman with showers,

    up the down elevator.

When the elevator stopped at **7**
an artist got on with a painting of heaven,
and a dentist with drills,
a doctor with pills,
a singer with trills,
a lawyer with wills,

a boilermaker,

and an undertaker,

    up the down elevator.

TOOLS

When the elevator stopped at **8**
a guard got on with a padlocked gate,
and a mover with a crate,
a fisherman with bait,
a governor with a state,

a pilot with a wing,
a bridegroom with a ring,
a crown upon a king,
a cowboy lassoing,
    up the down elevator.

When the elevator stopped at **9**
a lineman got on with a huge reel of line,
and a pigman with swine,
a vintner with wine,
a woodsman with a pine,
a painter with a sign,

a librarian,

a fruitarian,

a vegetarian,

a veterinarian,

    up the down elevator.

When the elevator stopped at **10**
a poet got on with a notebook and pen,
and a fireman with a hose,
a sculptor with a pose,
a chiropodist with toes,

a hunter with a deer,
a brewer with a beer,
an auctioneer,
an engineer,
a mountaineer,
and a musketeer with an old-fashioned gun.

Then they rode down together all the way to **1**
down the up elevator.